HAL•LEONARD®
GUITAR PLAY-ALONG

AUDIO ACCESS INCLUDED

VOL. 35

T0052886

Guitar in cover photograph provided by Mequon Music.

Tracking, mixing, and mastering by Jake Johnson
All guitars by Doug Boduch
Bass by Tom McGirr
Keyboards by Warren Wiegratz
Drums by Scott Schroedl

To access audio visit:
www.halleonard.com/mylibrary
Enter Code
3253-9384-6976-3178

ISBN 978-0-634-08399-0

HAL•LEONARD®

Visit Hal Leonard Online at
www.halleonard.com

Contact us:
Hal Leonard
7777 West Bluemound Road
Milwaukee, WI 53213
Email: info@halleonard.com

In Europe, contact:
Hal Leonard Europe Limited
42 Wigmore Street
Marylebone, London, W1U 2RN
Email: info@halleonardeurope.com

In Australia, contact:
Hal Leonard Australia Pty. Ltd.
4 Lentara Court
Cheltenham, Victoria, 3192 Australia
Email: info@halleonard.com.au

Guitar Notation Legend

THE MUSICAL STAFF shows pitches and rhythms and is divided by bar lines into measures. Pitches are named after the first seven letters of the alphabet.

TABLATURE graphically represents the guitar fingerboard. Each horizontal line represents a string, and each number represents a fret.

4th string, 2nd fret   1st & 2nd strings open, played together   open D chord

HALF-STEP BEND: Strike the note and bend up 1/2 step.

WHOLE-STEP BEND: Strike the note and bend up one step.

GRACE NOTE BEND: Strike the note and bend up as indicated. The first note does not take up any time.

SLIGHT (MICROTONE) BEND: Strike the note and bend up 1/4 step.

BEND AND RELEASE: Strike the note and bend up as indicated, then release back to the original note. Only the first note is struck.

PRE-BEND: Bend the note as indicated, then strike it.

VIBRATO: The string is vibrated by rapidly bending and releasing the note with the fretting hand.

PALM MUTING: The note is partially muted by the pick hand lightly touching the string(s) just before the bridge.

HAMMER-ON: Strike the first (lower) note with one finger, then sound the higher note (on the same string) with another finger by fretting it without picking.

PULL-OFF: Place both fingers on the notes to be sounded. Strike the first note and without picking, pull the finger off to sound the second (lower) note.

LEGATO SLIDE: Strike the first note and then slide the same fret-hand finger up or down to the second note. The second note is not struck.

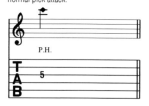

SHIFT SLIDE: Same as legato slide, except the second note is struck.

TRILL: Very rapidly alternate between the notes indicated by continuously hammering on and pulling off.

TAPPING: Hammer ("tap") the fret indicated with the pick-hand index or middle finger and pull off to the note fretted by the fret hand.

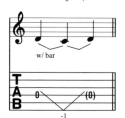

NATURAL HARMONIC: Strike the note while the fret-hand lightly touches the string directly over the fret indicated.

PINCH HARMONIC: The note is fretted normally and a harmonic is produced by adding the edge of the thumb or the tip of the index finger of the pick hand to the normal pick attack.

TREMOLO PICKING: The note is picked as rapidly and continuously as possible.

VIBRATO BAR DIVE AND RETURN: The pitch of the note or chord is dropped a specified number of steps (in rhythm) then returned to the original pitch.

VIBRATO BAR SCOOP: Depress the bar just before striking the note, then quickly release the bar.

VIBRATO BAR DIP: Strike the note and then immediately drop a specified number of steps, then release back to the original pitch.

Additional Musical Definitions

 (accent) • Accentuate note (play it louder)

 (staccato) • Play the note short

D.S. al Coda • Go back to the sign (𝄋), then play until the measure marked *"To Coda,"* then skip to the section labelled *"Coda."*

D.C. al Fine • Go back to the beginning of the song and play until the measure marked *"Fine"* (end).

Fill • Label used to identify a brief melodic figure which is to be inserted into the arrangement.

N.C. • Instrument is silent (drops out).

  • Repeat measures between signs.

  • When a repeated section has different endings, play the first ending only the first time and the second ending only the second time.

CONTENTS

Decadence Dance

Words and Music by Nuno Bettencourt and Gary Cherone

Tune down 1/2 step:
(low to high) Eb-Ab-Db-Gb-Bb-Eb

Intro

Moderate Rock ♩ = 134

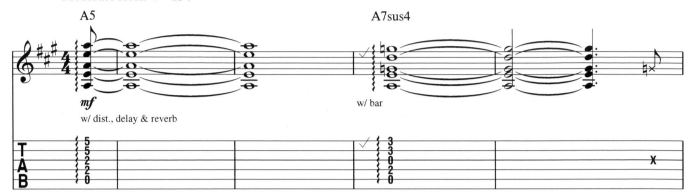

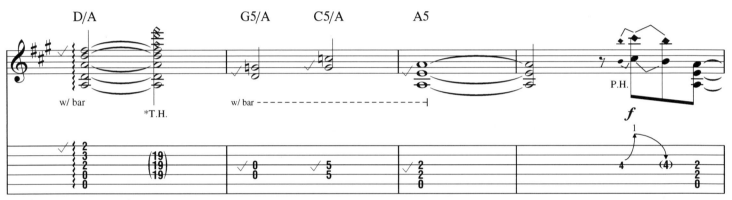

*Touch harmonic produced by lightly touching strings
w/ right hand while previous chord is still ringing.

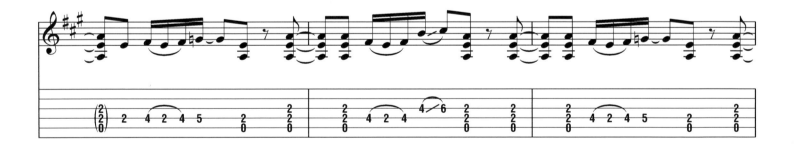

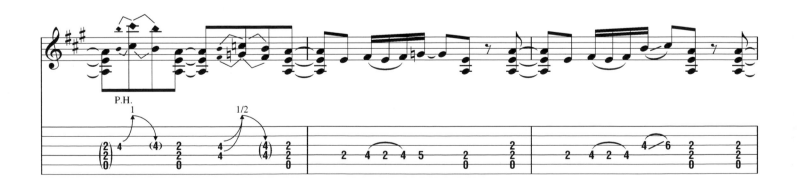

Let's go. ____

P.H.

Verse

G5   D5   A5   N.C.

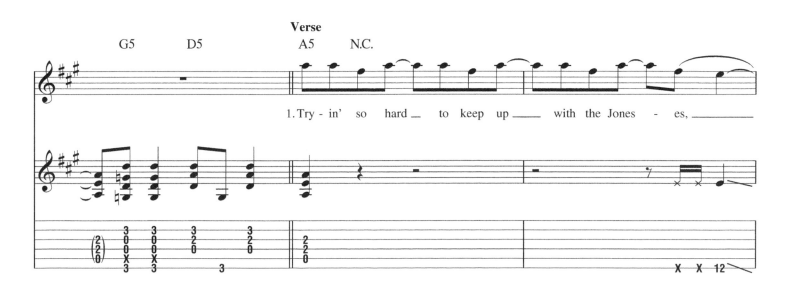

1. Try - in' so hard ___ to keep up ____ with the Jones - es, ____

*Pick behind nut.

8

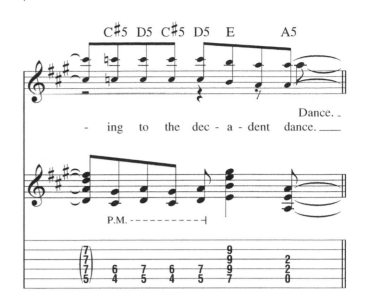

$\oplus$ **Coda**

Chorus

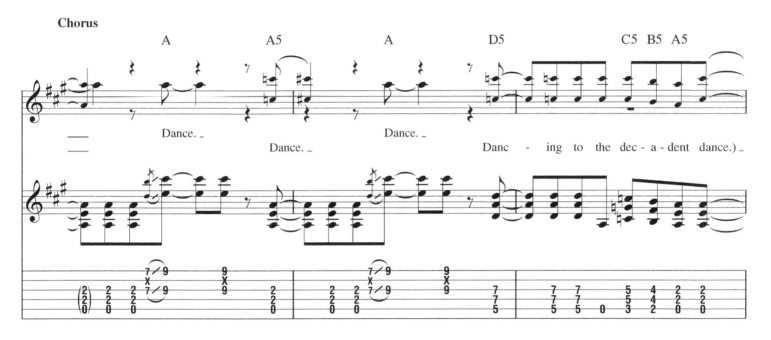

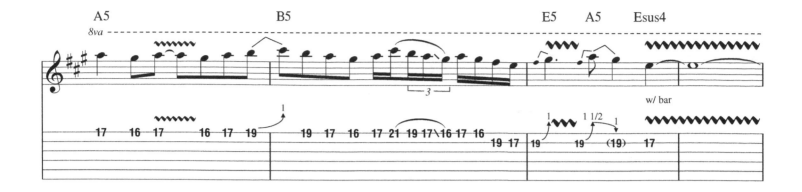

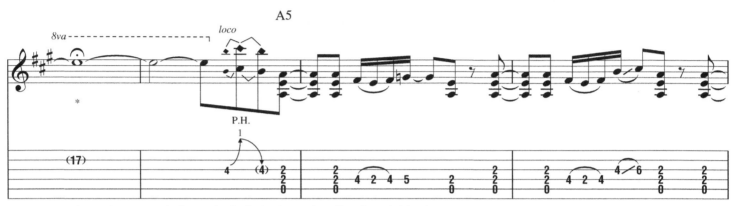

*Improvise over sustained note using feedback, whammy bar, glissandos and pick noises.

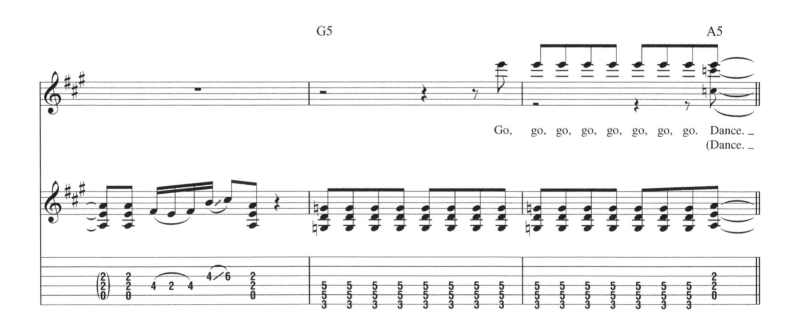

Go, go, go, go, go, go, go, go. Dance. _
(Dance. _

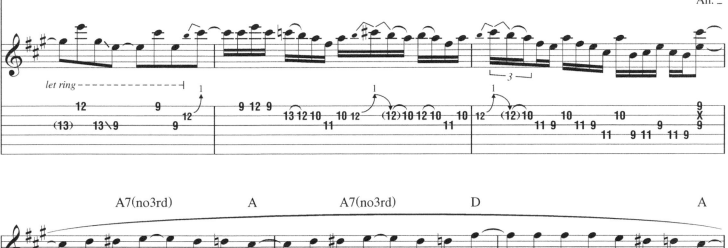

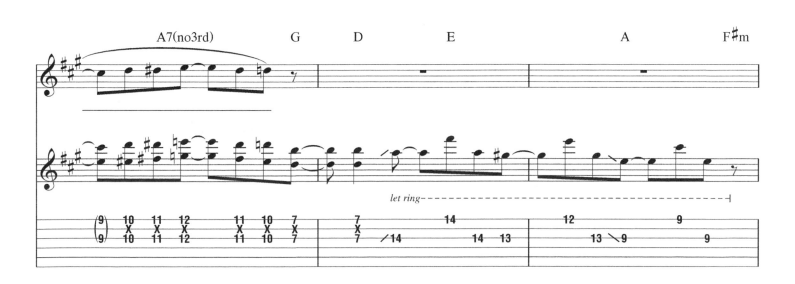

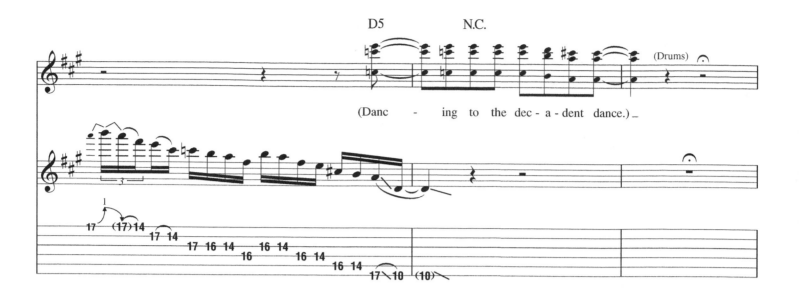

(Danc - ing to the dec - a - dent dance.)

Huh.

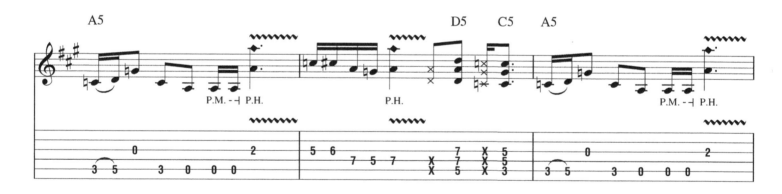

Pitch: E

Don't Treat Me Bad

Words and Music by Bill Leverty, Carl Snare, Michael Foster and Cosby Ellis

Tune down 1/2 step:
(low to high) Eb-Ab-Db-Gb-Bb-Eb

Intro

Moderately ♩ = 111

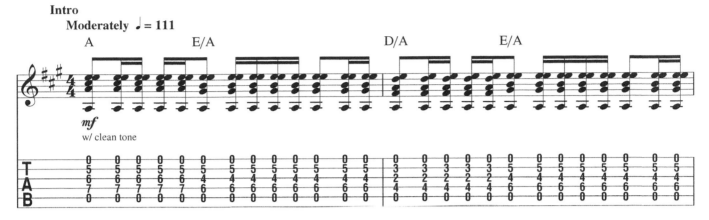

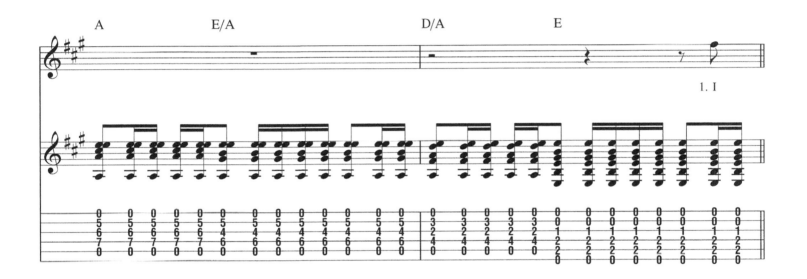

Verse

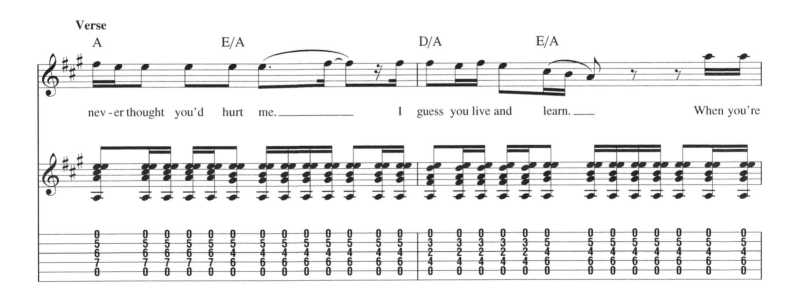

nev-er thought you'd hurt me.___ I guess you live and learn.___ When you're

To Coda 2

To Coda 1

Verse

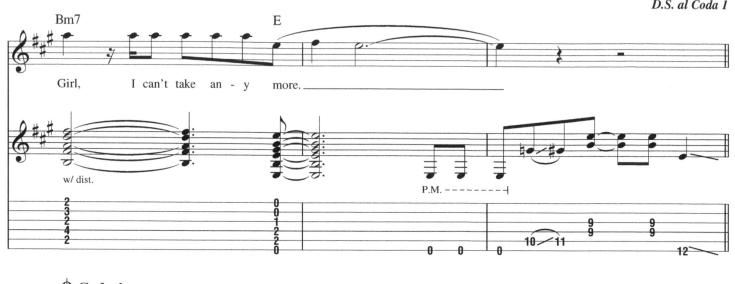

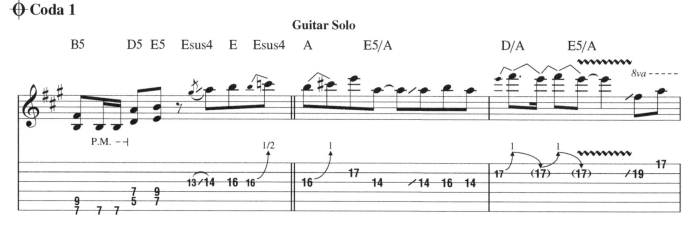

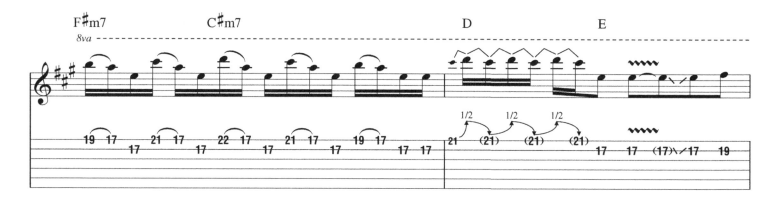

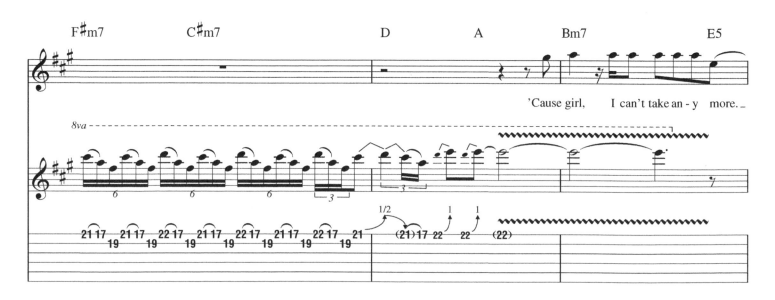

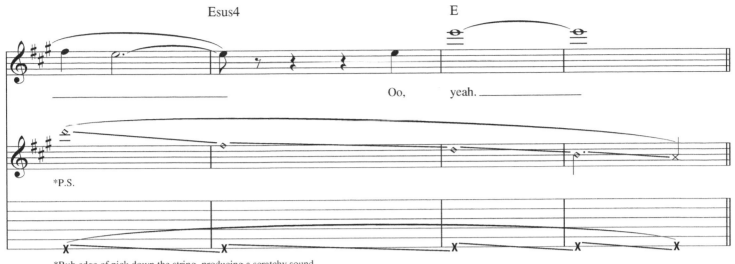

Esus4   E

Oo, yeah.

*P.S.

*Rub edge of pick down the string, producing a scratchy sound.

Interlude

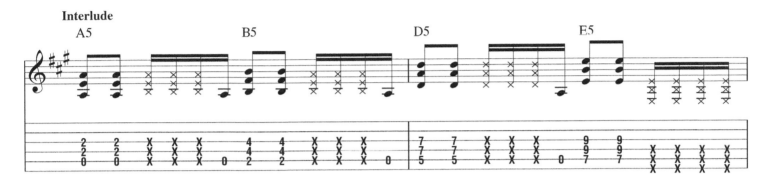

A5   B5   D5   E5

D.S. al Coda 2

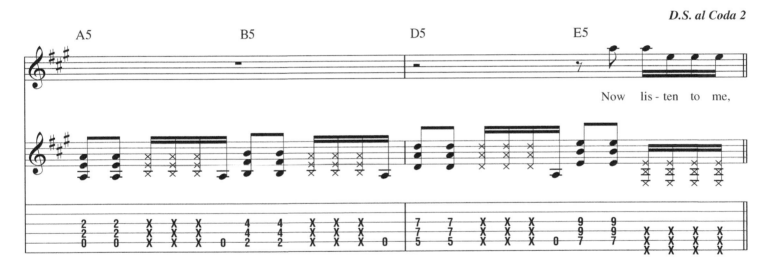

A5   B5   D5   E5

Now lis-ten to me,

Coda 2

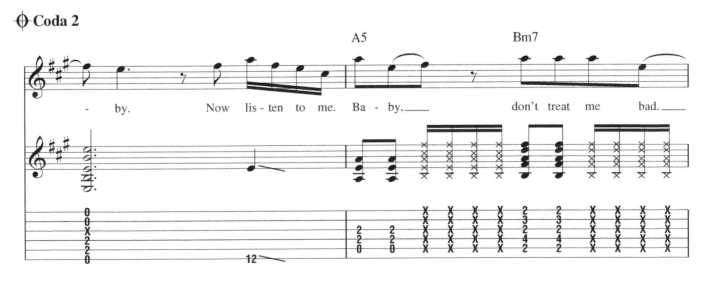

A5   Bm7

- by. Now lis-ten to me. Ba-by, don't treat me bad.

12

Down Boys

Words and Music by Jani Lane, Joey Allen, Jerry Dixon, Steven Sweet and Erik Turner

Tune down 1/2 step:
(low to high) E♭-A♭-D♭-G♭-B♭-E♭

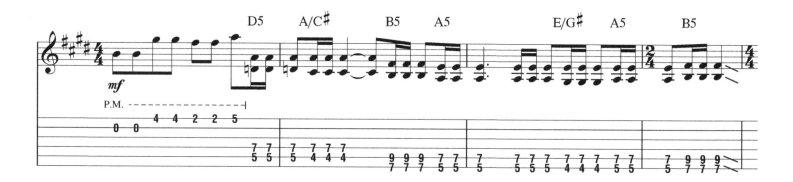

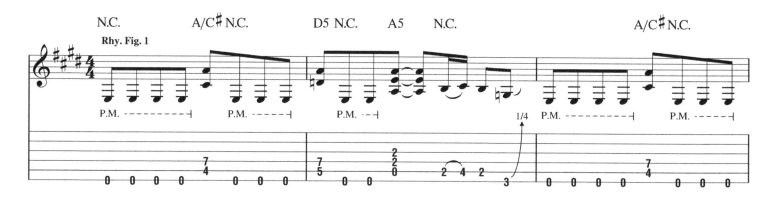

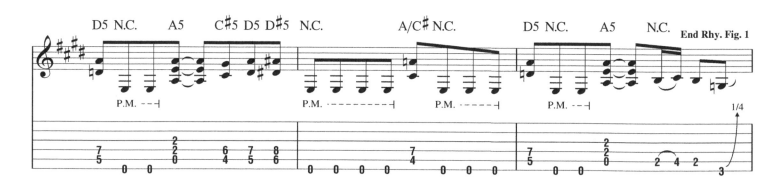

Pre-Chorus

Whoa.　Can we re-wind＿ to where we've been?　Oh, I wish you'd take a look　and

Harm.　w/ bar

Pitch: G

Chorus

2nd time, substitute Fill 2

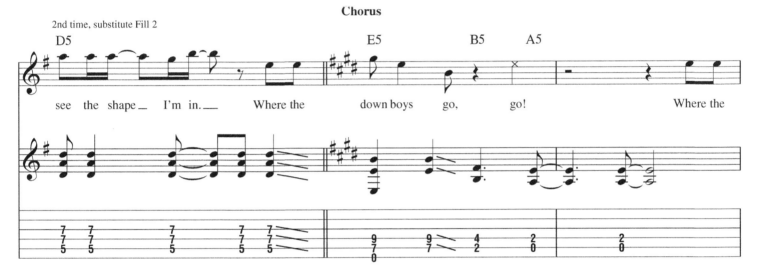

see the shape＿ I'm in.＿ Where the　　down boys　go,　go!　　Where the

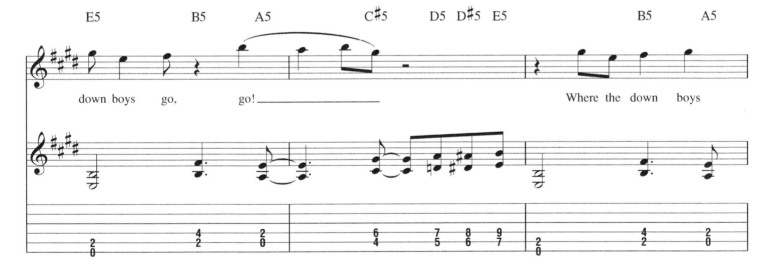

down boys　go,　　go!＿＿＿＿＿＿ Where the down　boys

Fill 2

go,___ yeah! I wan-na go where the down boys go,___ ba-by! down boys___ go, ba - by!

Guitar Solo

Pitch: C   D

*Strike note while bar is still depressed.

D.S. al Coda

**Strike harmonic while bar is still depressed.

Additional Lyrics

3. You comb your hair, put on your shades,
   You look real cool.
   You're giving me the runaround, make me feel like a fool.
   Got a lot of nerve to call me cheap, even though it's true.
   Now I don't care where we go tonight, take me along with you.

4. Some things you do really make me mad,
   I must confess.
   The way the streetlight silhouettes our things,
   Inside your dress,
   Oo, yeah.

Seventeen

Words and Music by Kip Winger, Reb Beach and Beau Hill

Tune down 1/2 step:
(low to high) E♭-A♭-D♭-G♭-B♭-E♭

Intro
Moderate Rock ♩ = 96

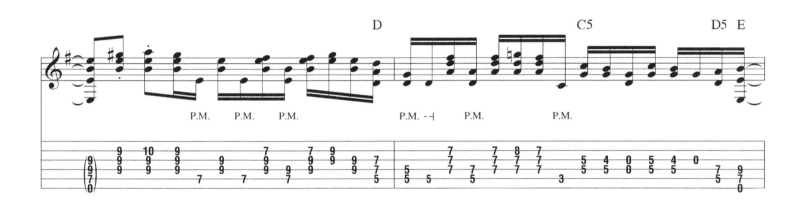

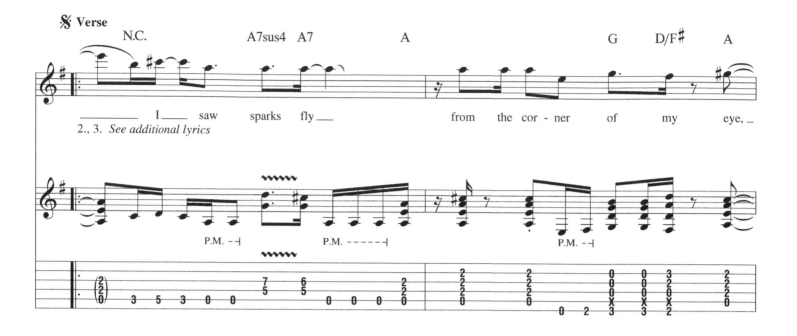

%S **Verse**

_____ I____ saw sparks fly ____ from the cor - ner of my eye, _

2., 3. See additional lyrics

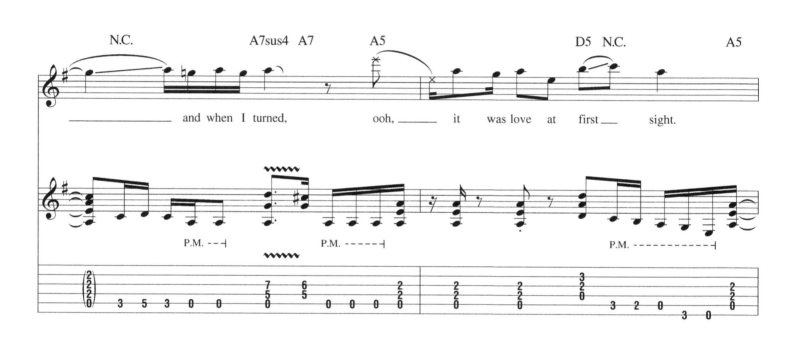

_____ and when I turned, ooh, _____ it was love at first ____ sight.

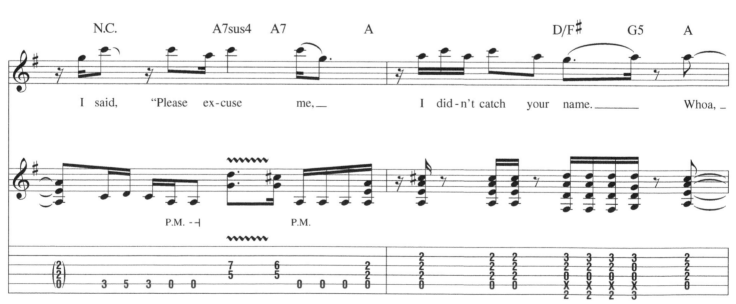

I said, "Please ex-cuse me, __ I did-n't catch your name. _____ Whoa, _

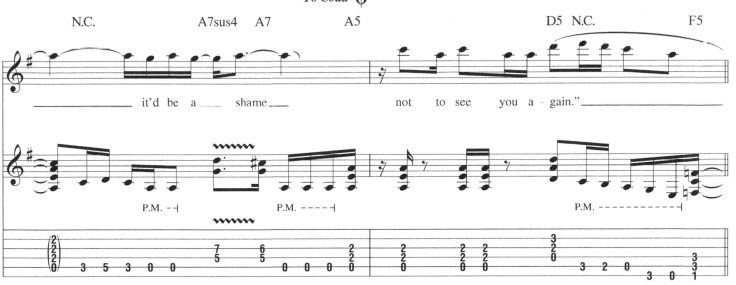

Pre-Chorus

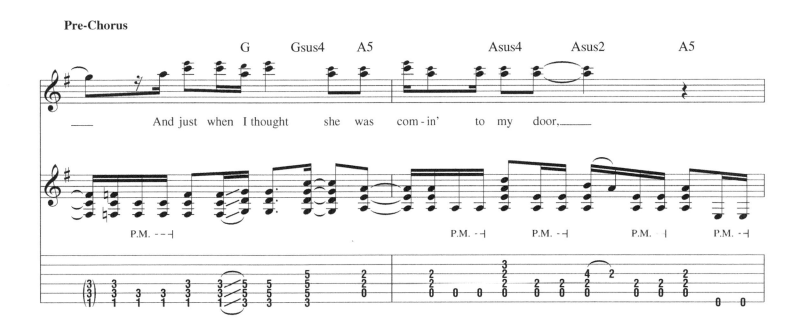

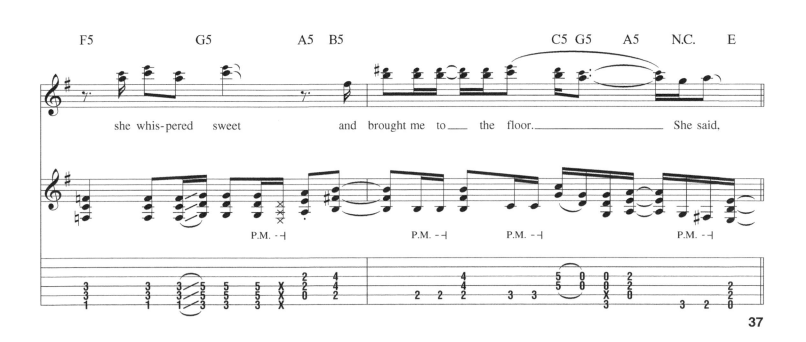

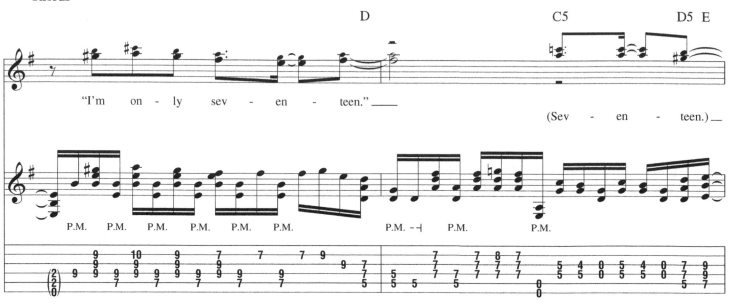

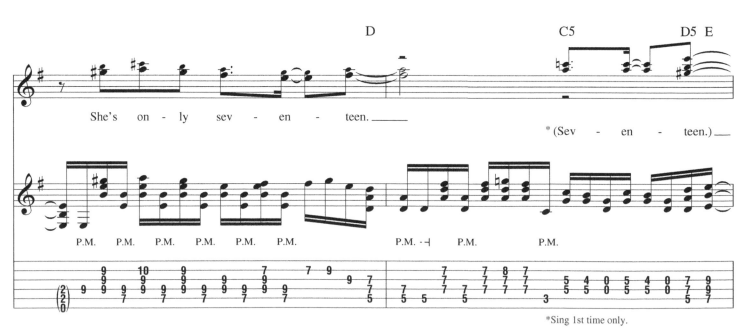

*Sing 1st time only.

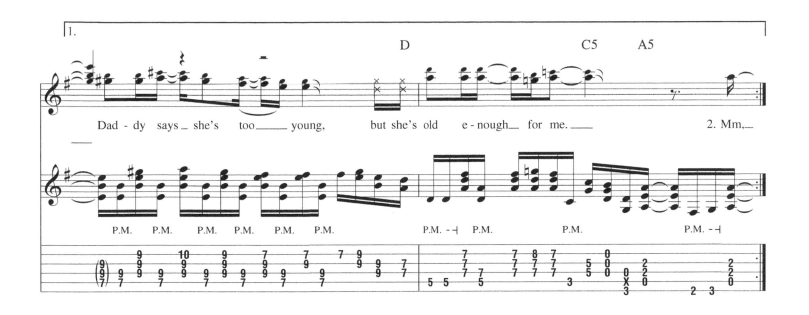

Dad - dy says _ she's too _____ young, but she's old e - nough _ for me. _____ 2. Mm,___

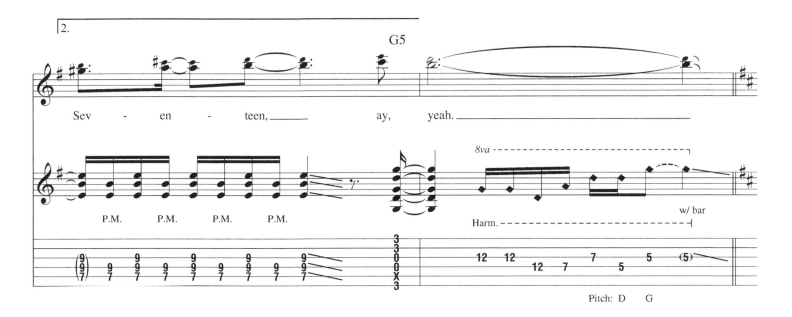

Sev - - en - teen, _____ ay, yeah. _____

Pitch: D   G

Guitar Solo

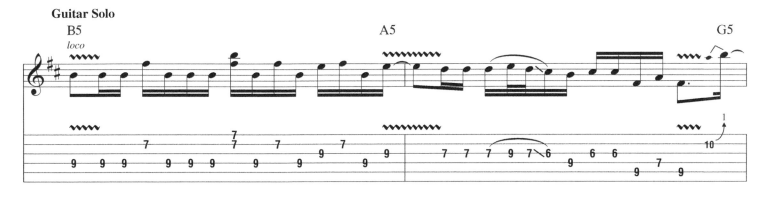

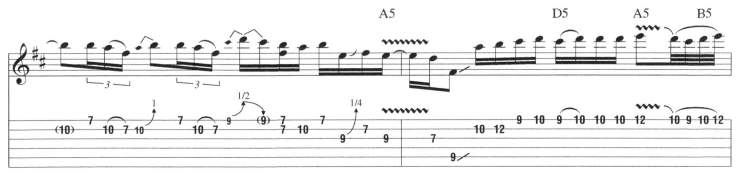

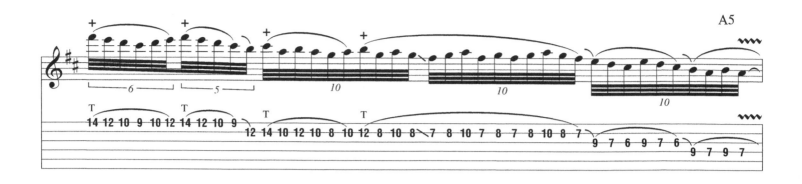

A5

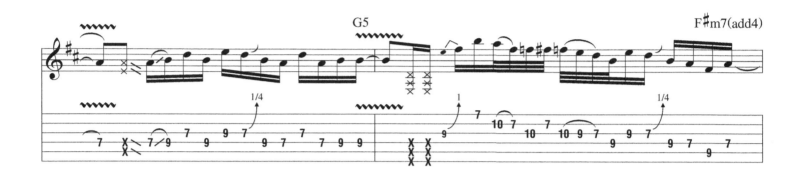

G5　　　　　　　　　　　　　　　　　　F♯m7(add4)

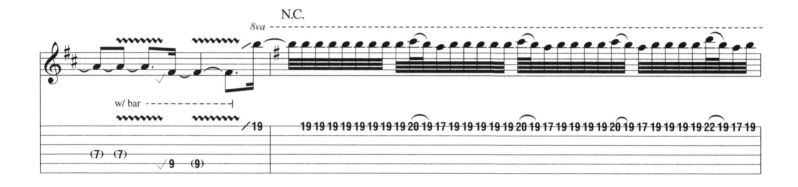

N.C.

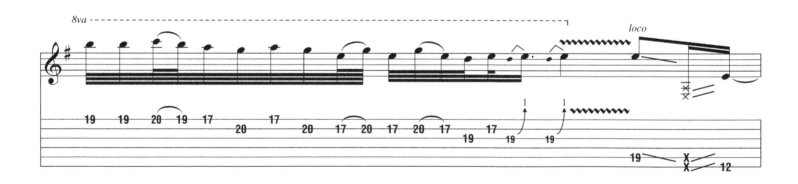

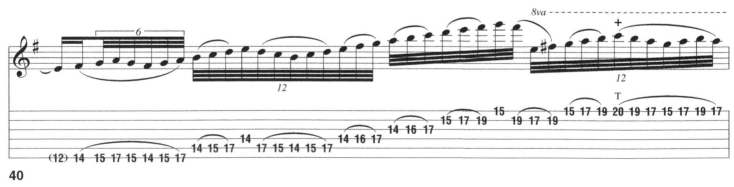

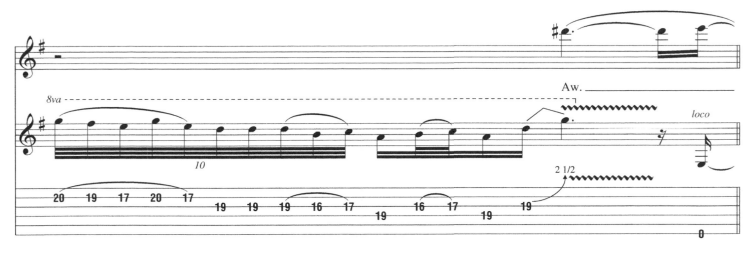

Interlude

D.S. al Coda

Coda

It must be love. _____ She's on-ly sev-en-teen. __

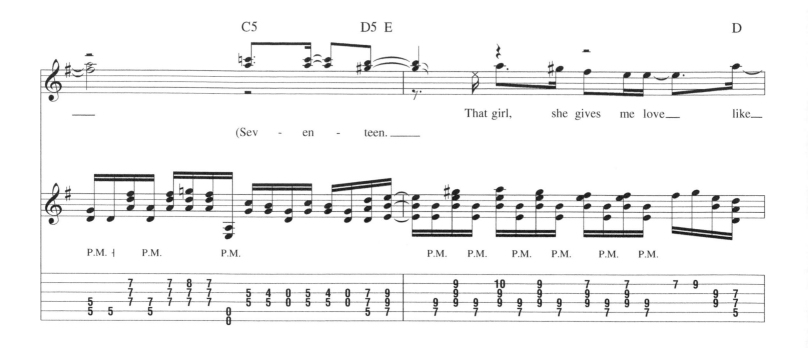

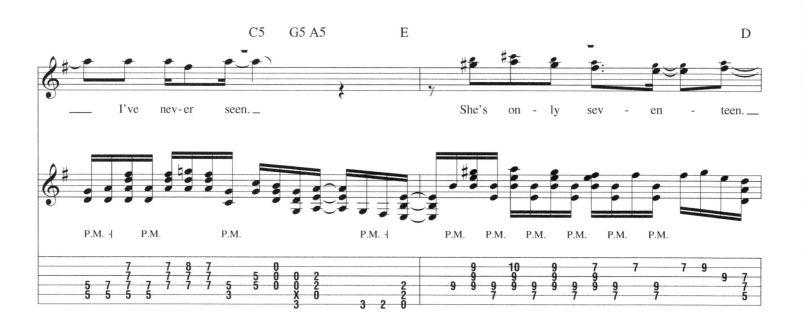

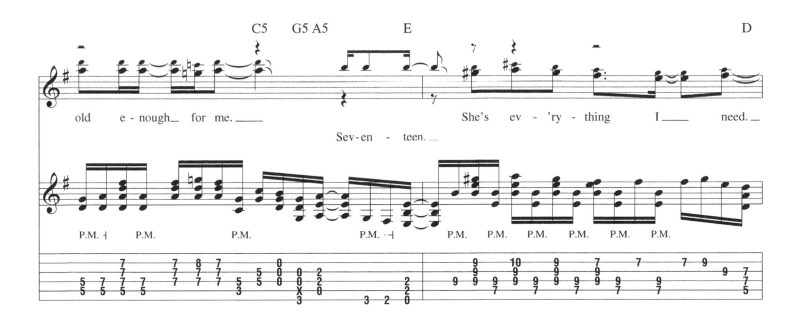

old e-nough_ for me. _____ She's ev-'ry-thing I_____ need. _____

Sev-en - teen.

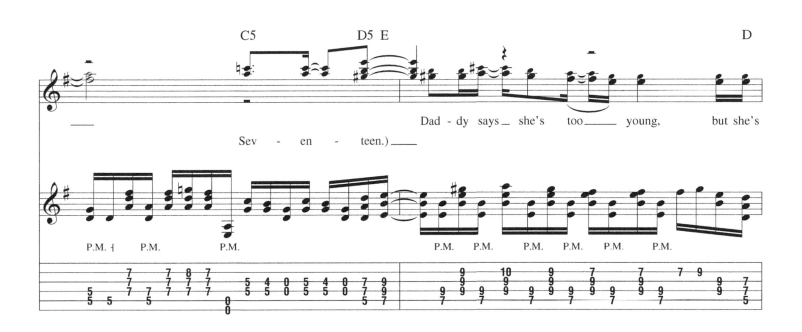

Dad - dy says_ she's too_____ young, but she's

Sev - en - teen.)_____

Outro-Guitar Solo

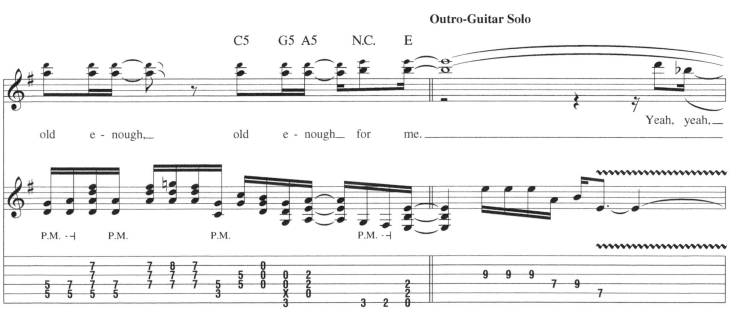

old e-nough,_ old e-nough_ for me. _____

Yeah, yeah,_____

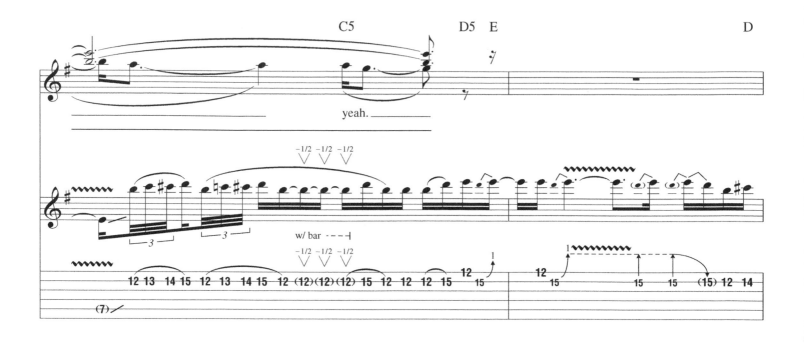

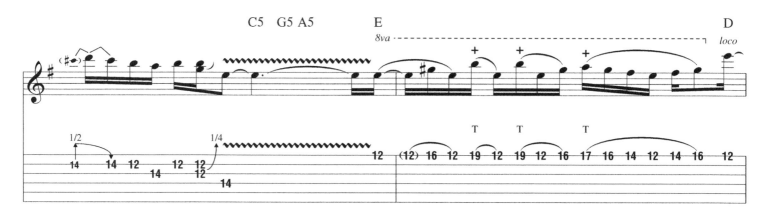

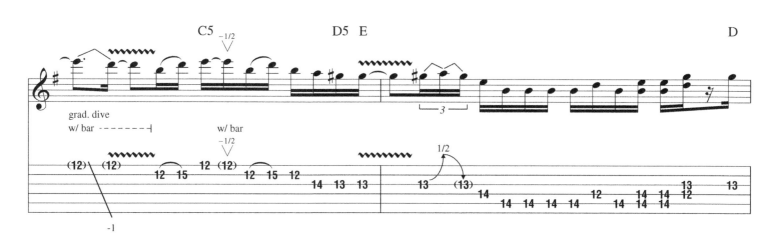

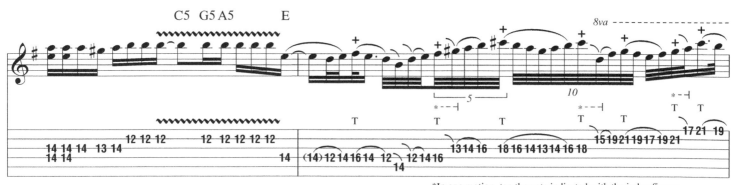

*In one motion, tap the note indicated with the index finger
of the pick hand, then pluck the adjacent string with the same
finger while pulling off.

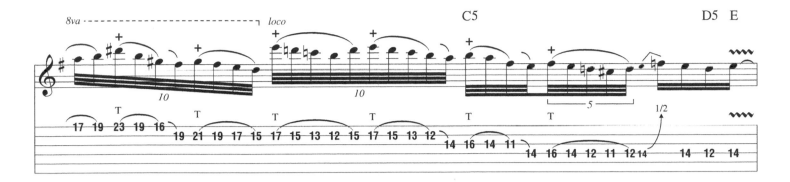

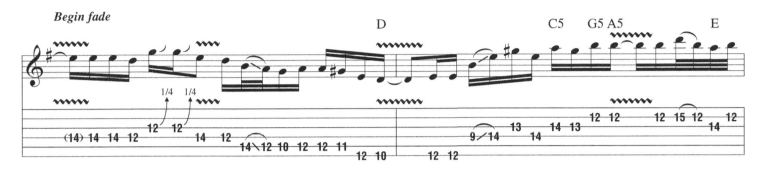

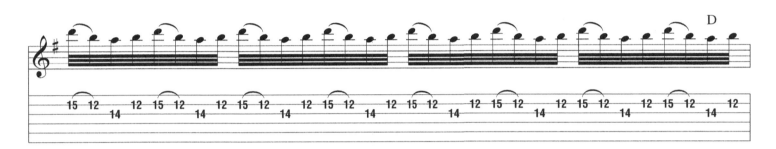

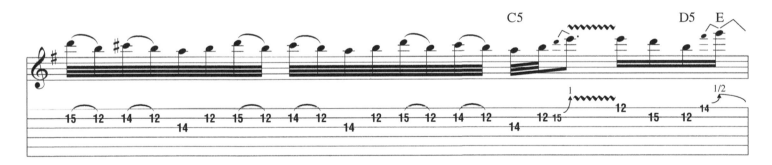

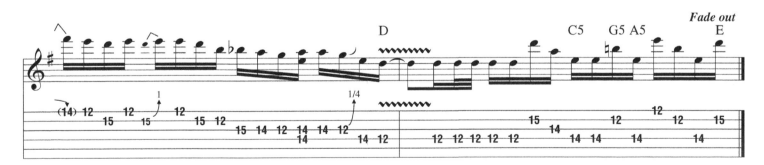

Additional Lyrics

2. Mm, come to my place; we can talk it over, oh,
Ev'rything going down in your head.
She says, "Take it easy, I need some time.
Time to work it out, to make you mine."

3. Yeah, such a bad girl, loves to work me overtime.
Feels good, hah, dancing close to the borderline.
She's a magic mountain, she's a leather glove.
Oh, she's my soul. It must be love.

Shake Me

Words and Music by Tom Keifer

Intro
Moderate Rock ♩ = 135

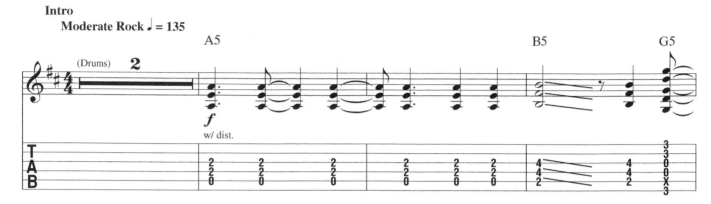

All right, — yeah.

Verse

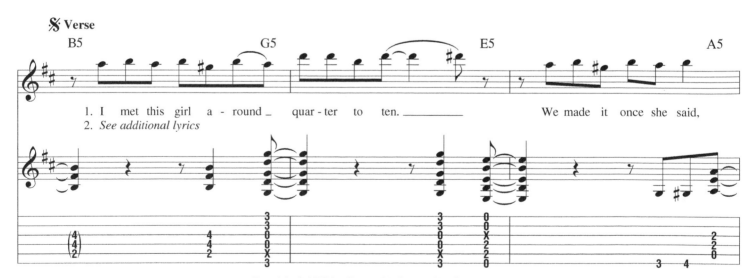

1. I met this girl a-round — quar-ter to ten. _____ We made it once she said,
2. *See additional lyrics*

Coda 1

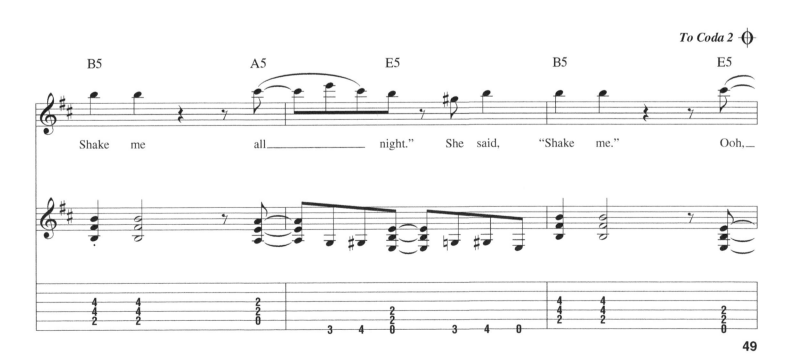

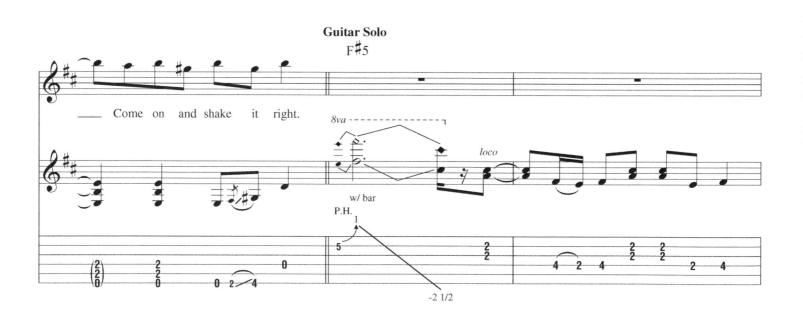

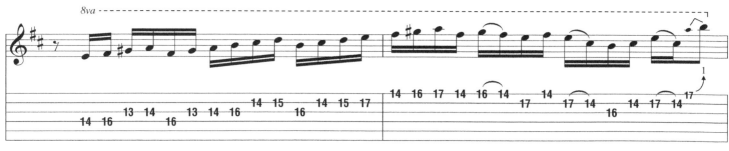

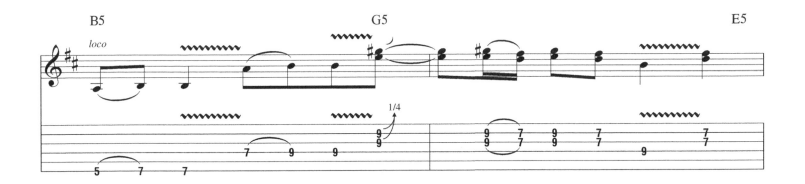

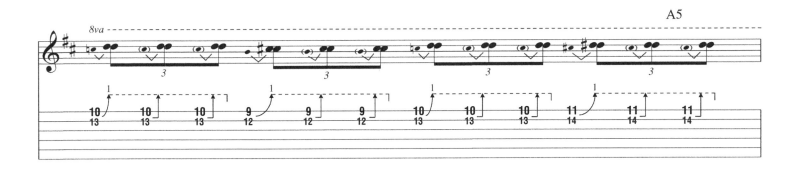

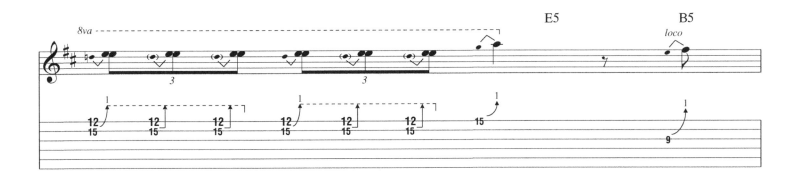

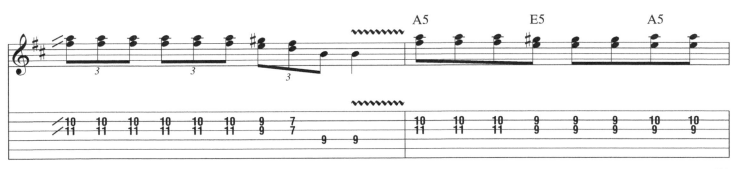

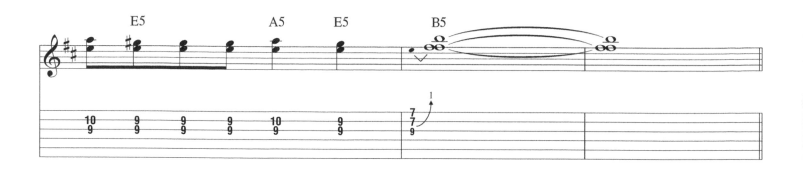

Interlude

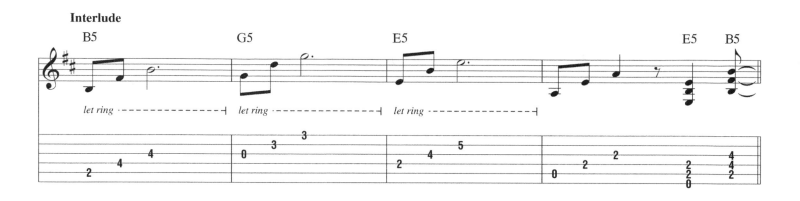

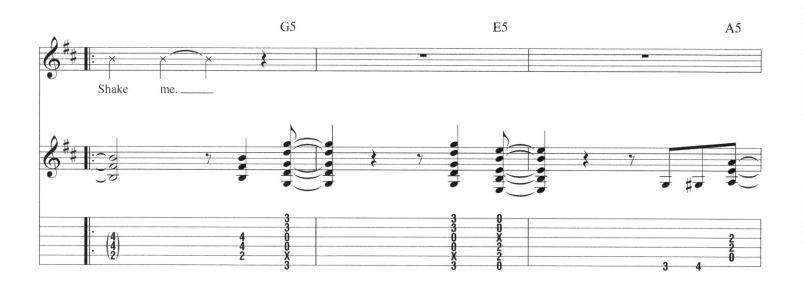

Shake me. ____

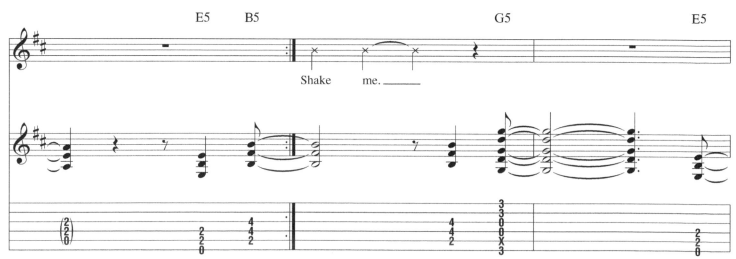

Shake me. ____

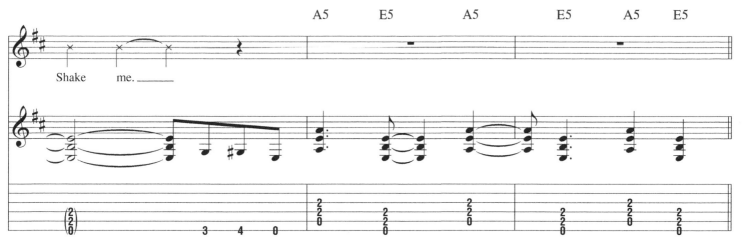

Shake me. ____

A5 E5 A5 E5 A5 E5

⊕ Coda 2

Outro-Guitar Solo

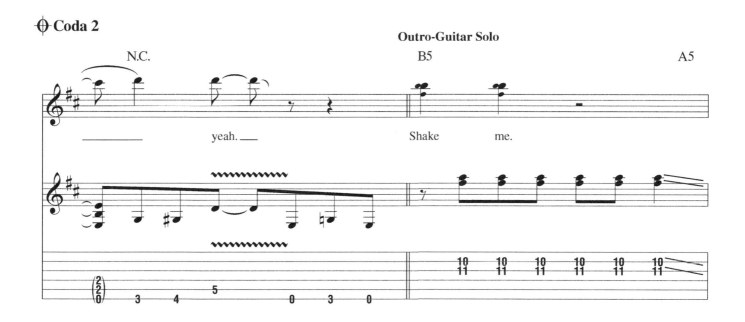

N.C.   B5   A5

____ yeah. ____   Shake   me.

Begin fade

E5   B5   E5   N.C.

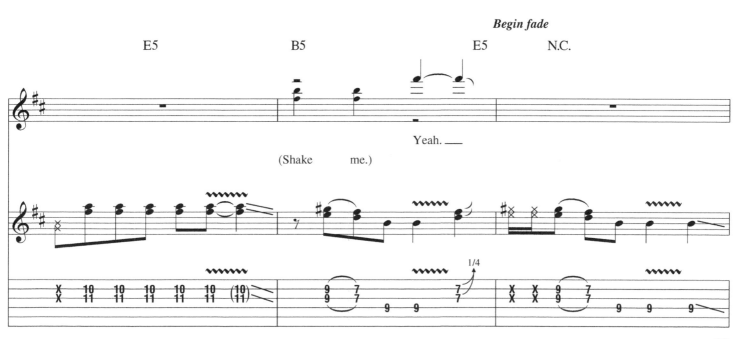

Yeah. ____

(Shake   me.)

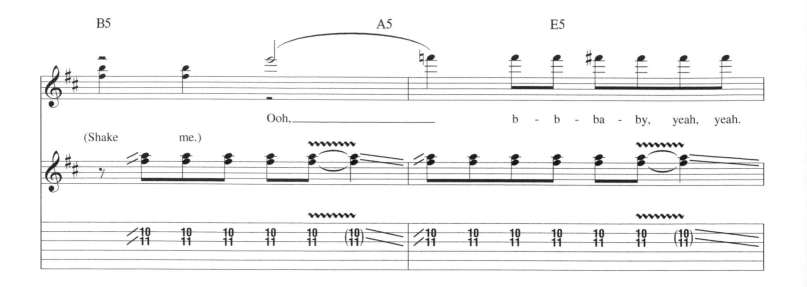

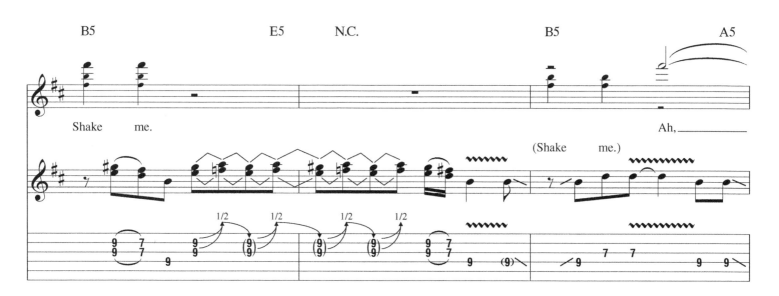

Additional Lyrics

2. Screamed and scratched and rolled out of the bed,
I never really got her out of my head.
And now and then she makes those social calls,
Gives me a squeeze, gets me kickin' the walls.
Now let me tell ya, it still feels tight,
And we were shakin' after every bite.
I feel her comin' in the middle of the night,
Screamin' higher.

Up All Night

Words and Music by Mark Slaughter and Dana Strum

Tune down 1 step:
(low to high) D-G-C-F-A-D

Intro
Moderately

Up all night, sleep all day. —

*Vol. swell (Gradually increase vol. over the next 4 meas.)

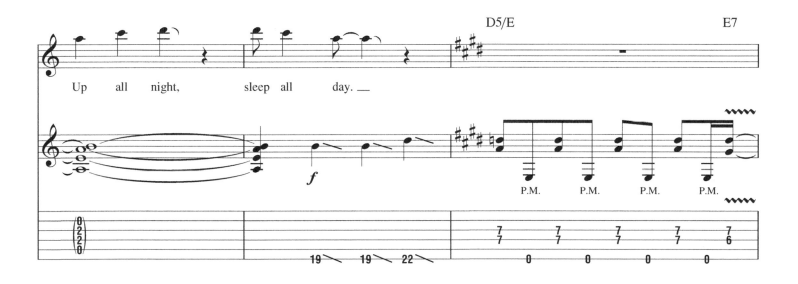

Up all night, sleep all day. —

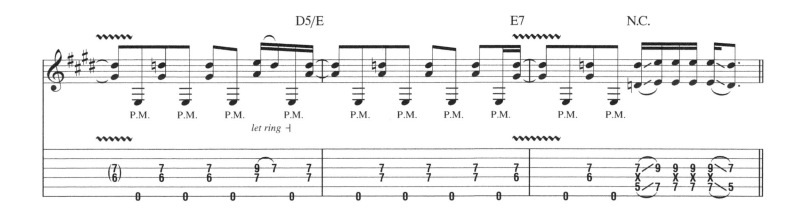

% Verse

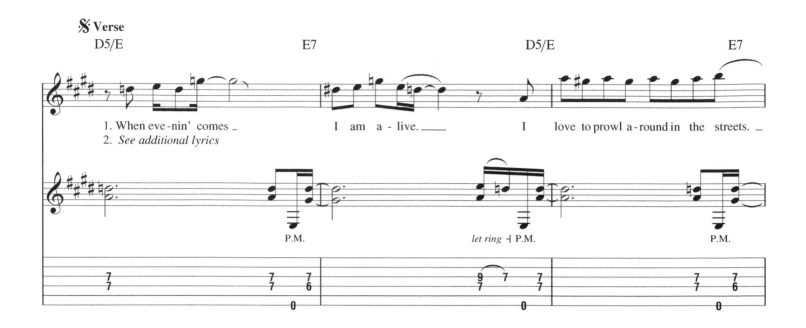

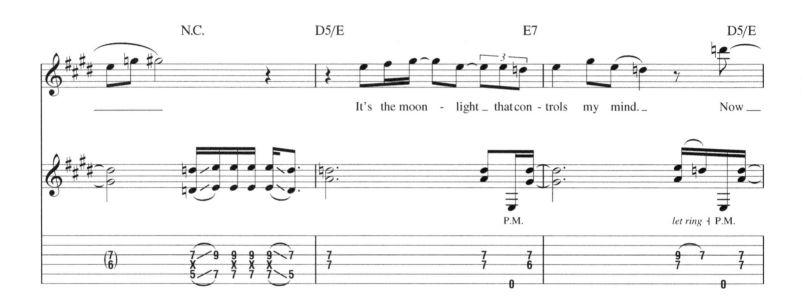

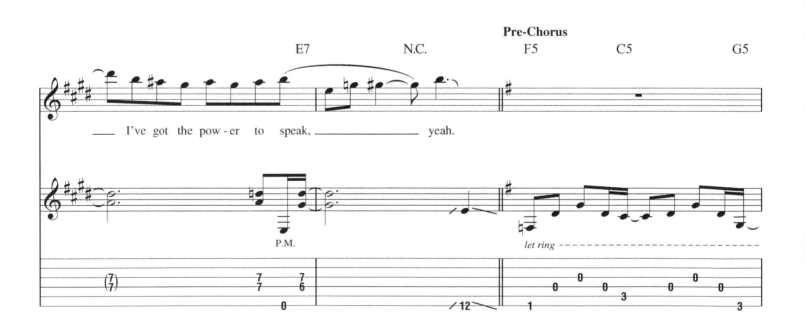

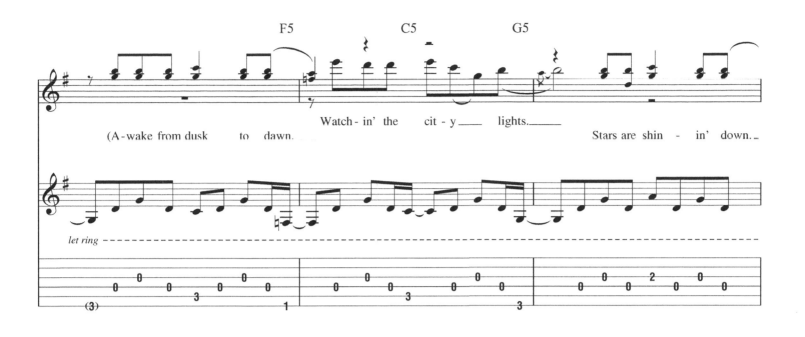

F5   C5   G5

(A-wake from dusk to dawn.   Watch-in' the cit-y___ lights.___   Stars are shin - in' down.___

F5   C5   G5   F5   C5   G5

They'll be shin-in' down on   you and I.   And I'll   hold you till the morn-in'___ light.___
___   And when morn - ing comes.) ___

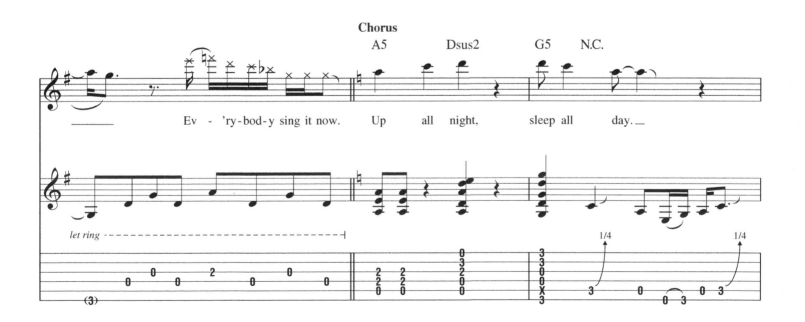

Chorus

A5   Dsus2   G5   N.C.

___   Ev - 'ry-bod-y sing it now.   Up   all   night,   sleep all   day. ___

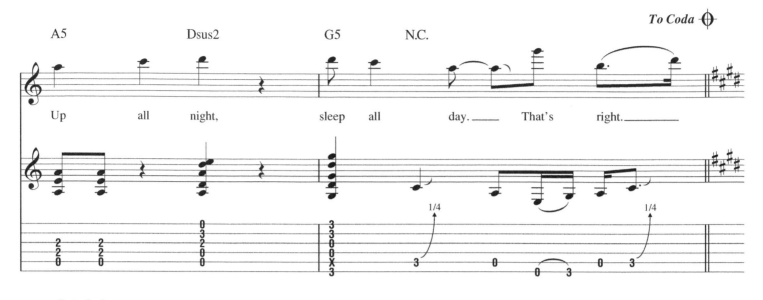

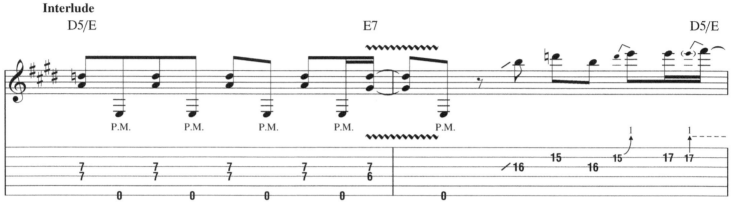

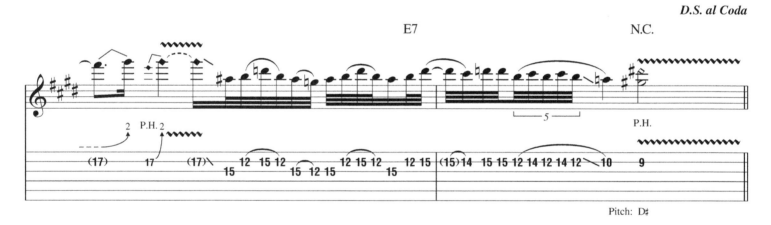

G5

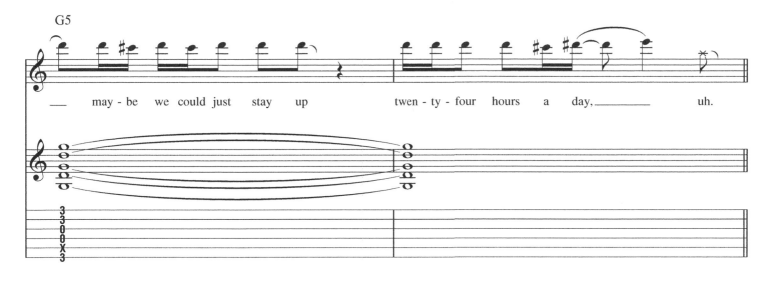

— may - be we could just stay up twen - ty - four hours a day,_____ uh.

Interlude

N.C.

Huh!

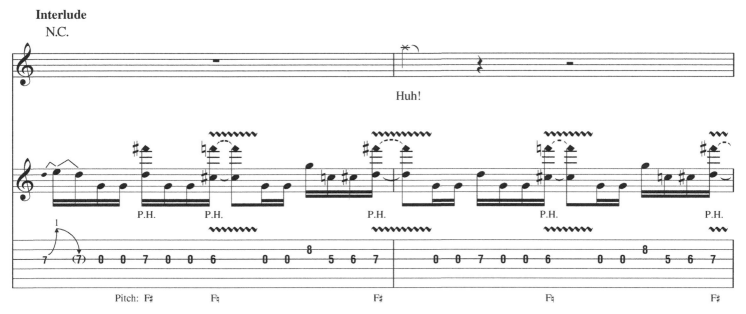

Pitch: F♯ F♮ F♯ F♮ F♯

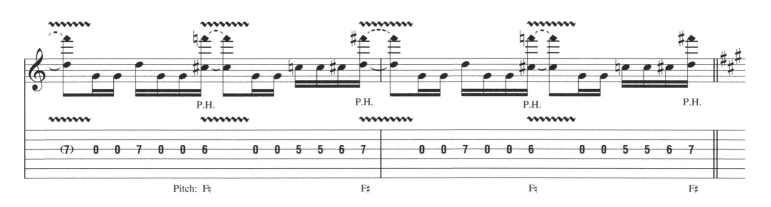

Pitch: F♮ F♯ F♮ F♯

Guitar Solo

F♯m Fmaj7♯11 G6

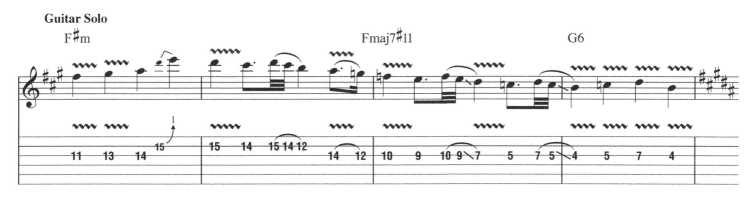

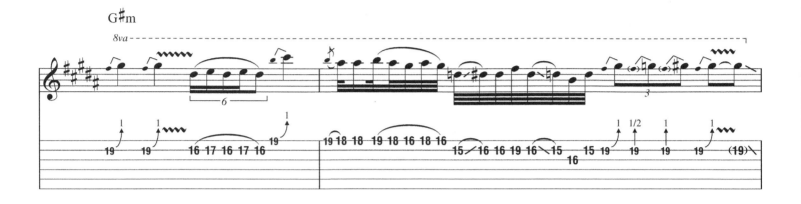

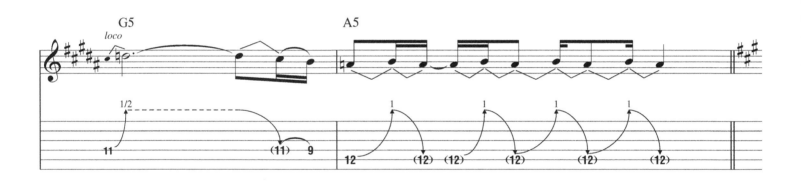

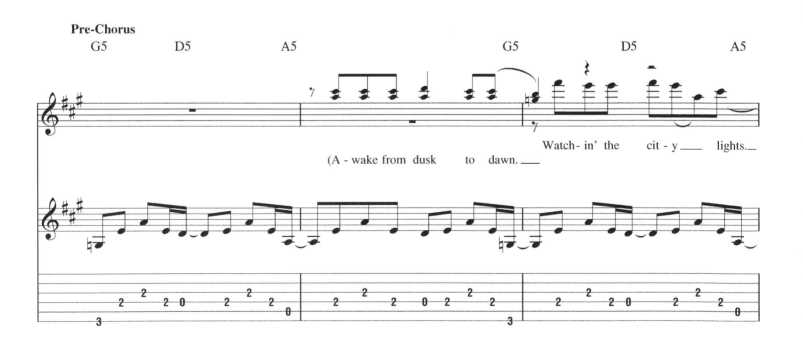

Additional Lyrics

2. Drivin' down the boulevard, all alone.
   The neon signs are callin' your name.
   Find me in the corner havin' the time of my life.
   You'd think you'd want to do the same.

Talk Dirty to Me

Words and Music by Bobby Dall, Brett Michaels, Bruce Anthony Johannesson and Rikki Rockett

Tune down 1/2 step:
(low to high) Eb-Ab-Db-Gb-Bb-Eb

Intro

Moderately fast ♩ = 124

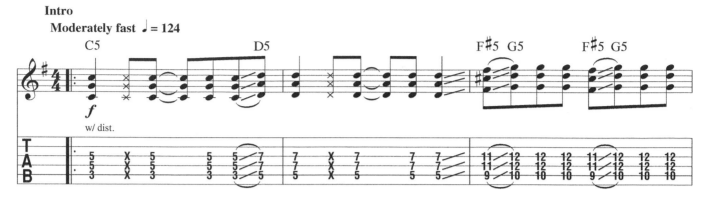

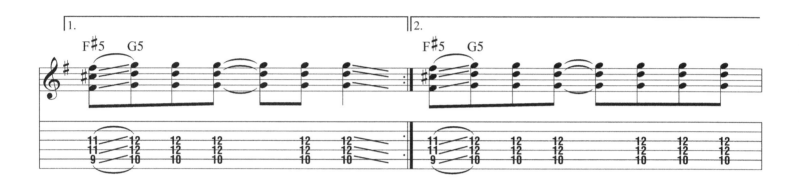

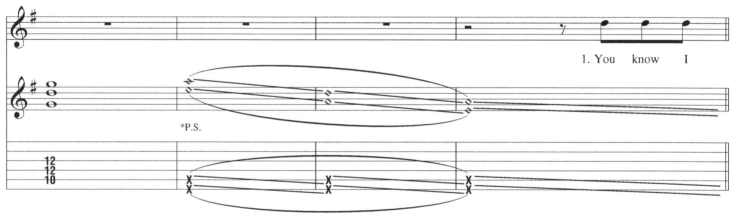

*Rub edge of pick down the strings, producing a scratchy sound.

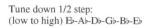

nev- er,   I nev- er seen you look so good, ___ you

D5

nev - er act the way you should, ___ uh, but I like ___

C5

___ it. And I know you like it too, ___

G5

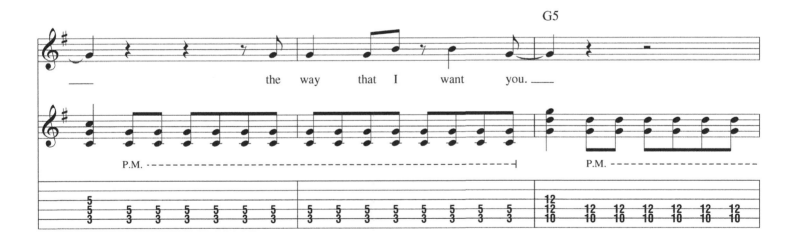

the way that I want you. ___

D

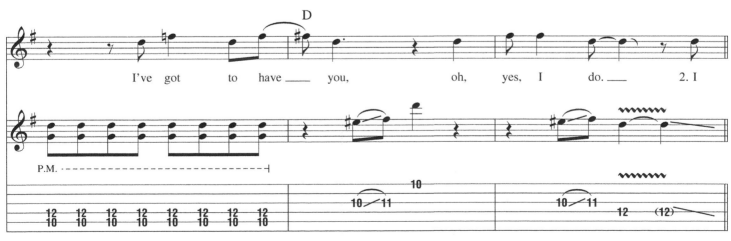

I've got to have ___ you, oh, yes, I do. ___ 2. I

Verse

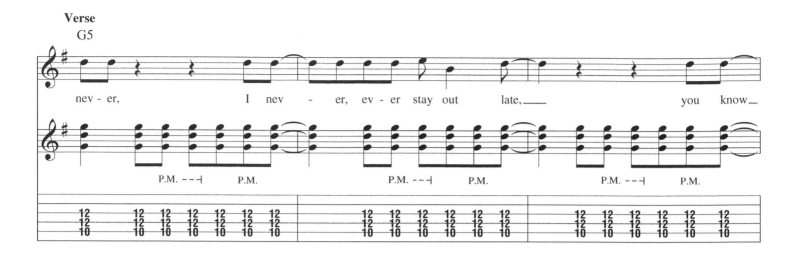

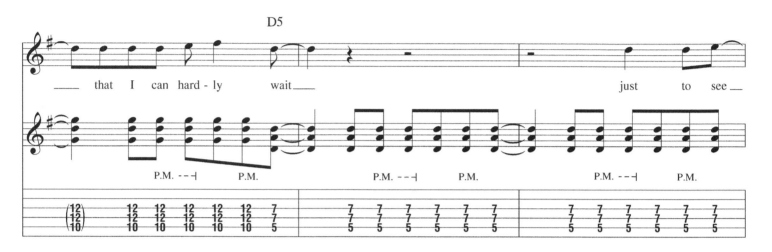

I got - ta touch___ you.   'Cause ba - by, we'll___ be___

%· **Chorus**

3rd time, substitute Fill 1

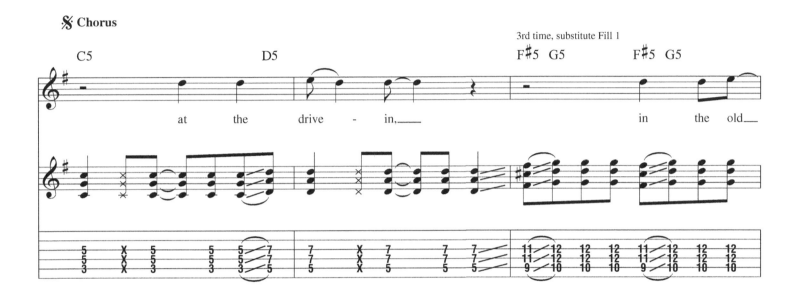

at the drive - in,___   in the old___

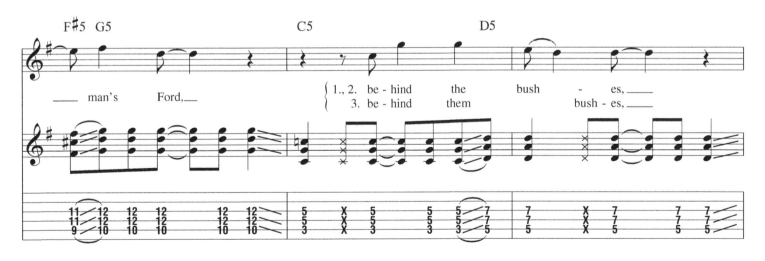

___ man's   Ford,___   1., 2. be - hind   the   bush - es, ___
                               3. be - hind   them   bush - es, ___

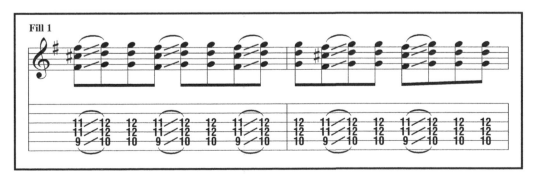

Fill 1

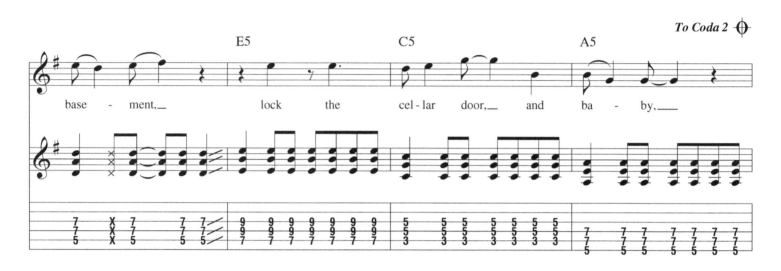

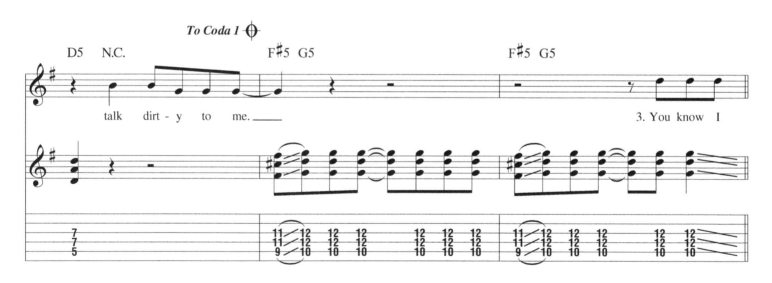

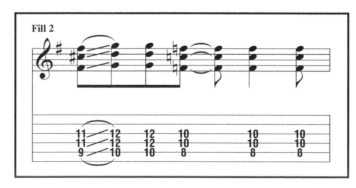

Verse

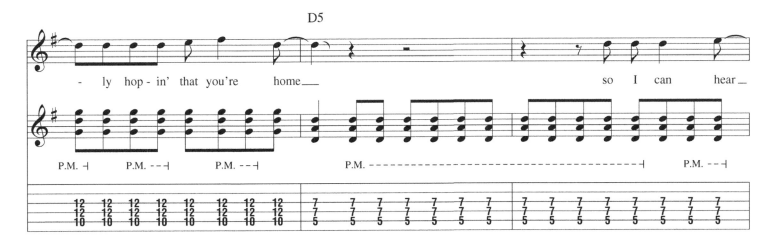

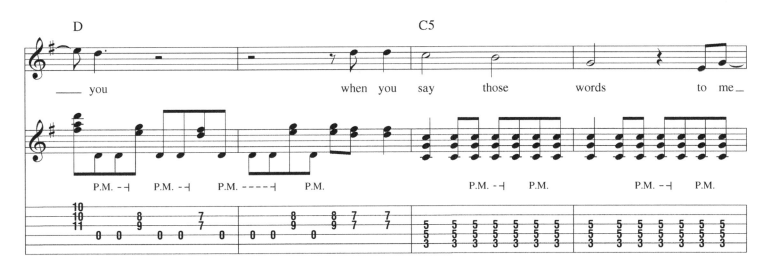

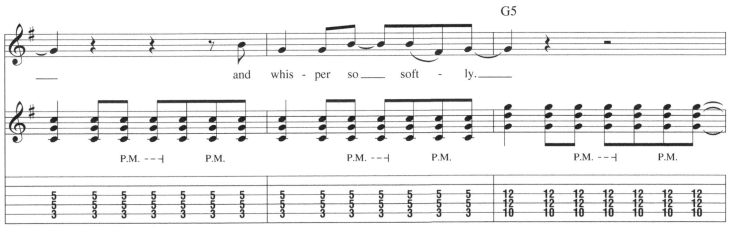

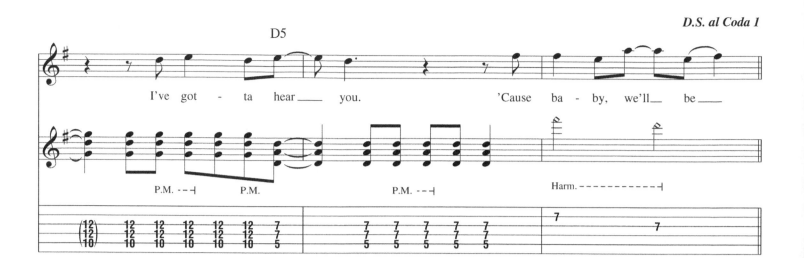

Coda 1

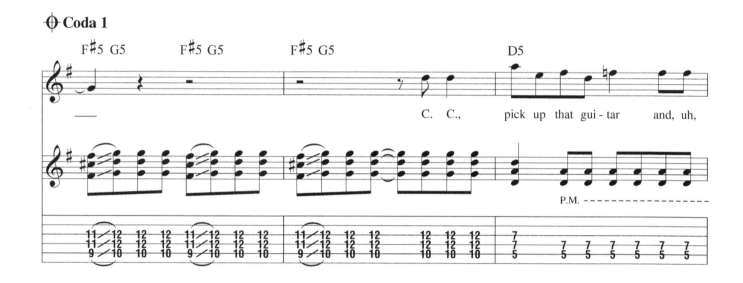

Guitar Solo

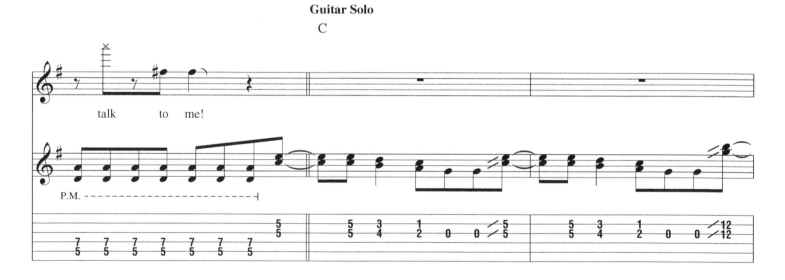

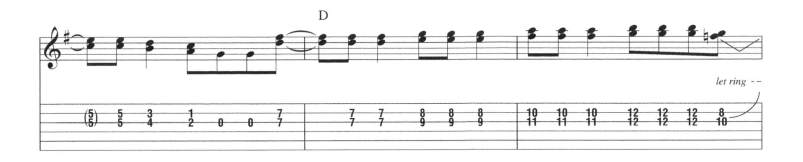

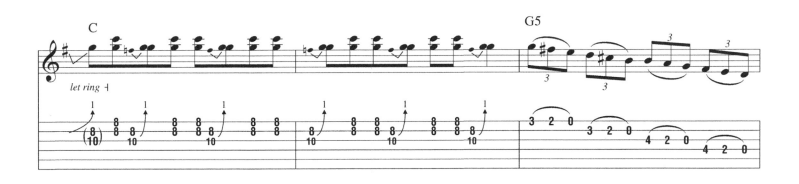

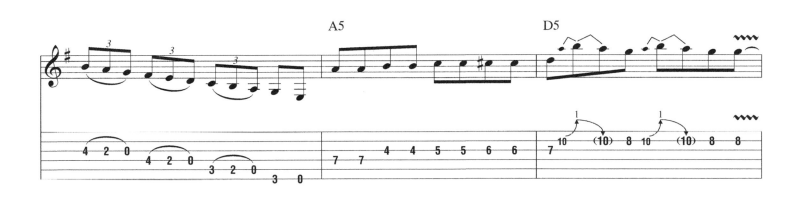

D.S. al Coda 2

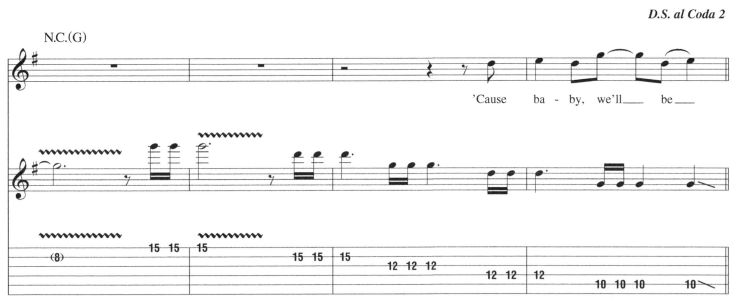

'Cause ba - by, we'll___ be___

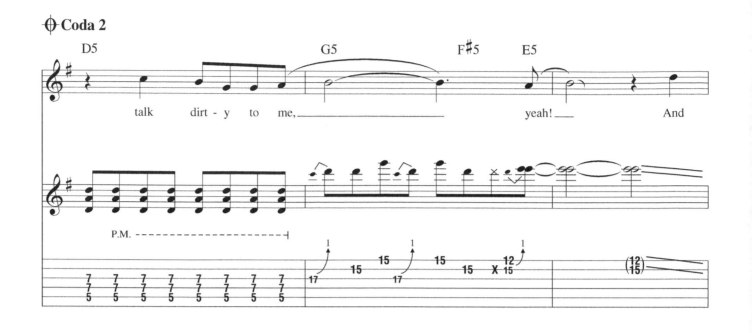

talk dirt-y to me, _____ yeah! _____ And

ba - by, _____ talk dirt-y to me, _____ yeah, yeah, yeah,

yeah. And ba - by, _____ talk dirt-y to me.

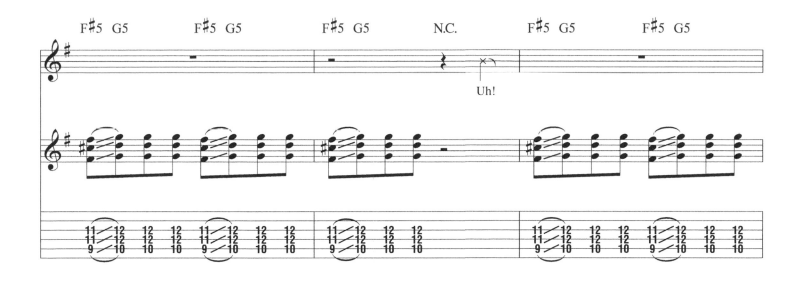

Free time

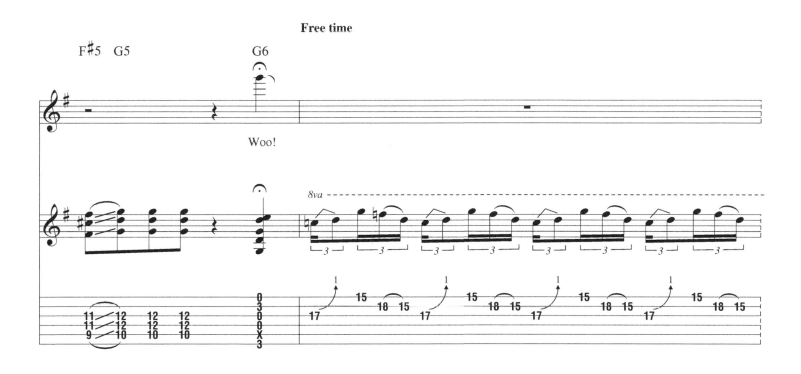

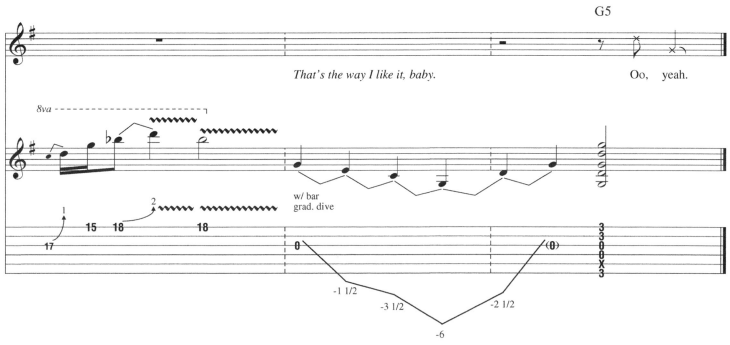

Wait

Words and Music by Mike Tramp and Vito Bratta

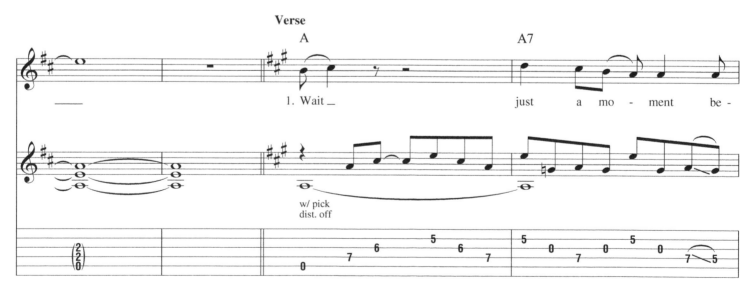

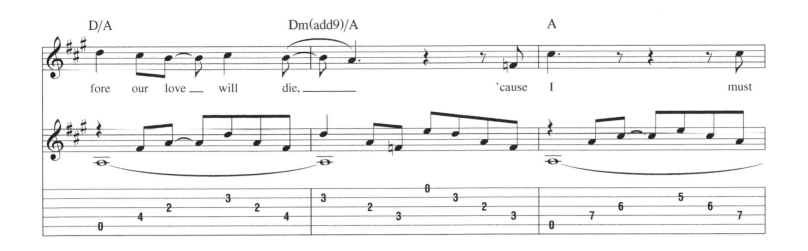

fore our love — will die, _____ 'cause I must

know the rea - son why ___ we say ___ good - bye. _____ I

Wait _ just a mo - ment and tell me ___ why, _____

_____ 'cause I ___ can show you lov - in' that _

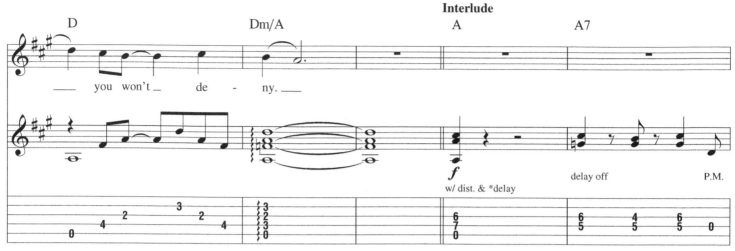

*Set for quarter-note regeneration w/ 3 repeats.

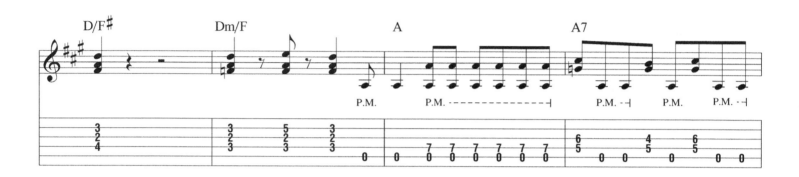

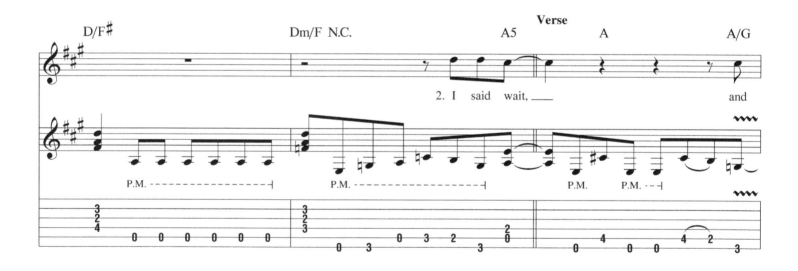

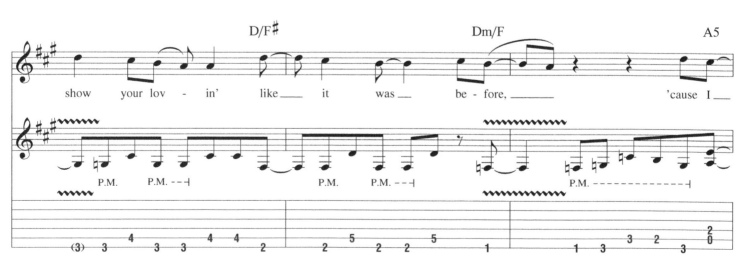

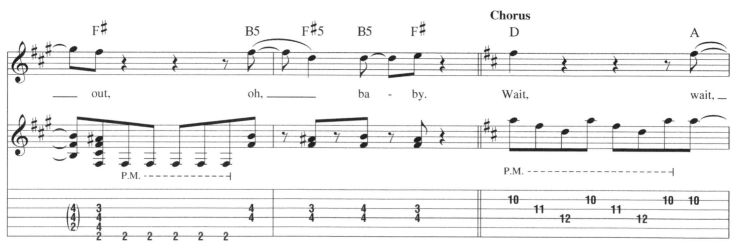

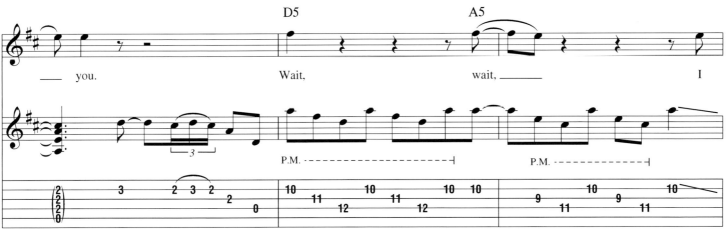

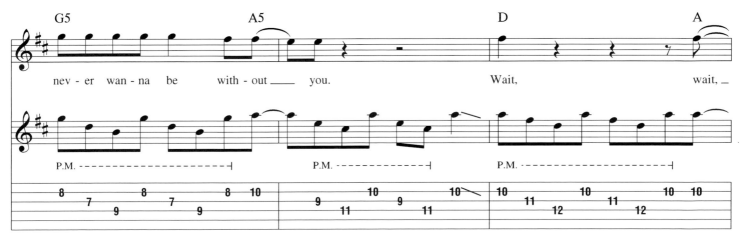

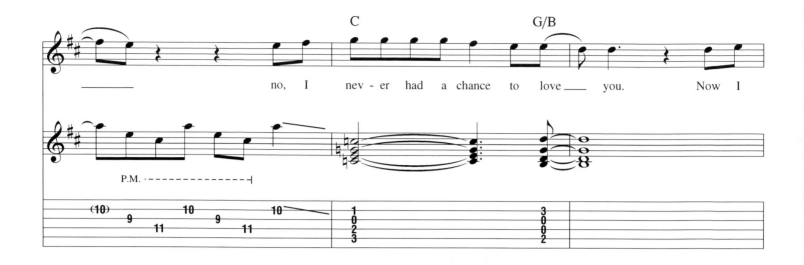

no, I nev- er had a chance to love____ you. Now I

on- ly wan- na say I love____ you one more time.____

Guitar Solo

*Bend and vibrato are executed by left hand, fingered at 3rd str., 2nd fr.

**Bend w/ left hand, at 3rd str., 9th fr.

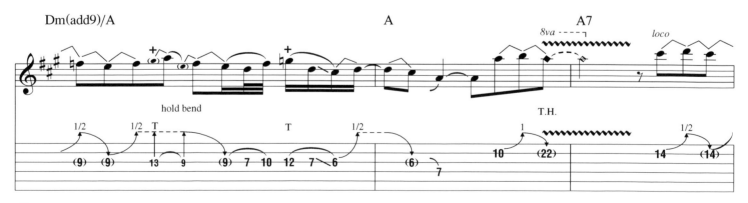

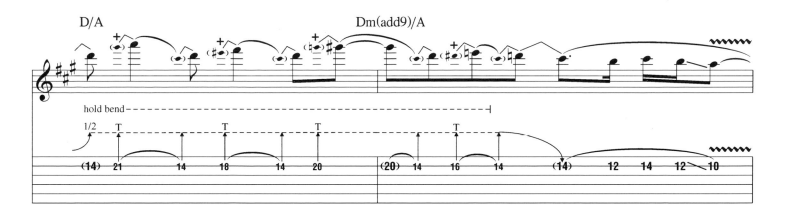

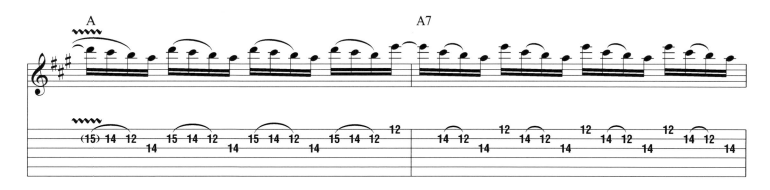

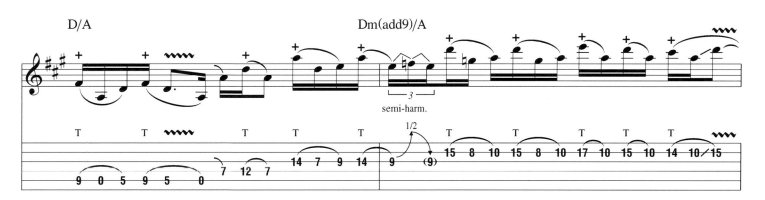

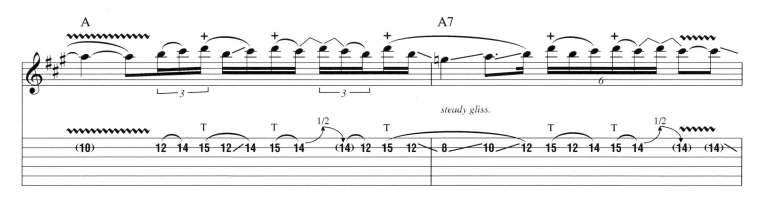

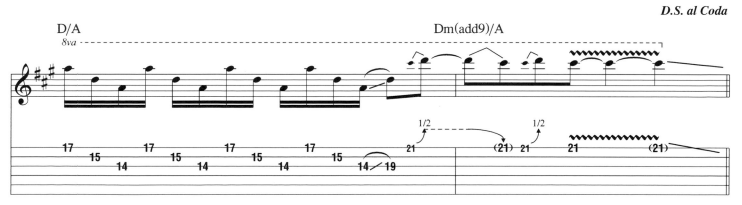

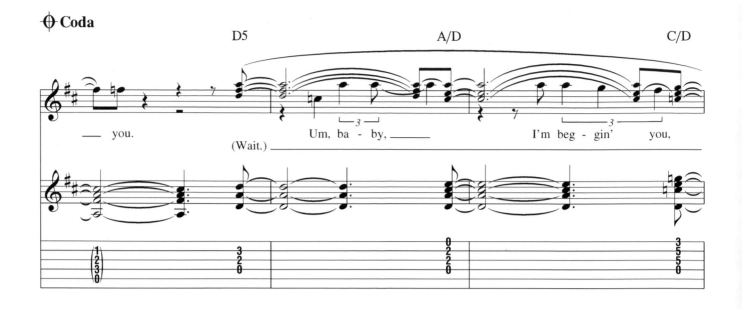

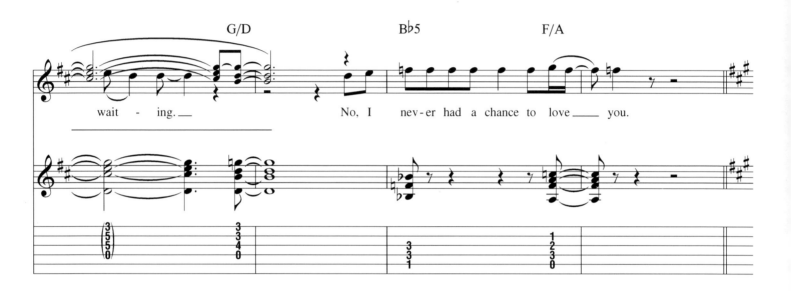

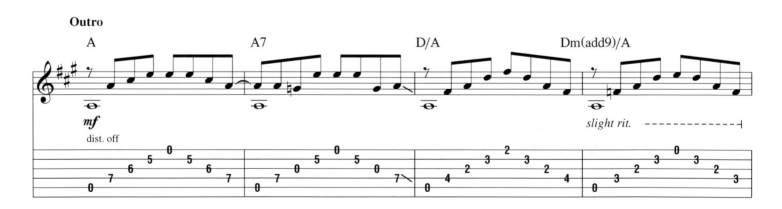

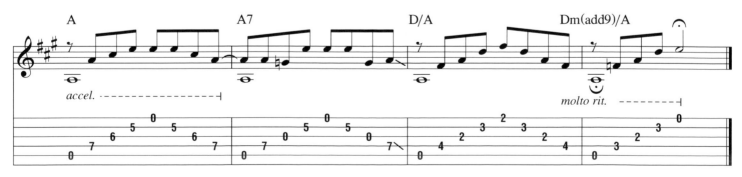